SWEET DESSERT FOR YOUR SOUL
Encouraging Lessons from God About Life

Paperback ISBN: 978-1-949297-76-8
Hardback ISBN: 978-1-949297-81-2
LCCN: 2022913641

Address all personal correspondence to:
Paula Douglas Ministries
Post Office Box 607
Hemingway, SC 29554
www.pauladouglas.org
info@pauladouglas.org
Individuals and church groups may order books from Paula Douglas directly, or from the publisher. Retailers and wholesalers should order from our distributors. Refer to the Deeper Revelation Books website for distribution information, as well as an online catalog of all our books.

Published by:
Deeper Revelation Books
Revealing "the deep things of God" (1 Cor. 2:10)
P.O. Box 4260
Cleveland, TN 37320 423-478-2843
Website: www.deeperrevelationbooks.org
Email: info@deeperrevelationbooks.org

Deeper Revelation Books assists Christian authors in publishing and dis¬tributing their books. Final responsibility for design, content, permissions, editorial accuracy, and doctrinal views, either expressed or implied, belongs to our authors. It is an honor and a joy for us to help our authors produce works of excellence for the glory of God and the advance of His kingdom.

Table of Contents

Introduction

My friend, Julia, asked me to write for her monthly publication.

I agreed.

Each month, I would sit with my laptop and think about what had been going on in my life and what life lesson I could extract from it to share with others.

Month after month, I would open my heart and pray that the Holy Spirit would reveal to me what experiences I needed to share with my readers as I journeyed on this bumpy road called life.

With child-like faith, the Lord diligently answered my prayers. Like a miracle, time after time, another article would be written, printed, and filed.

Several months into this experience, I began to notice that my writing seemed like a conversation between friends more than anything else. Nothing fancy. Just a convo' between two close friends.

Well, here we are, years later.

My file is now filled with hand-written notes on scraps of paper, inspiring, colorful pictures of all kinds of decadent desserts, and printed pages of completed thoughts about life. Joy and happiness, hurts, and disappointments are all included for the readers as I reveal the life lessons I have learned.

And now I have some new friends who are joining the conversation.

Together we will always share a scripture and maybe even ask a question or two.

So, grab a slice of cake and a cup of tea because you and I have things to talk about.

Friends do that you know.

From my lil' acre, with Miss Kitty, lovingly known as 'the farm.'

– Paula

Winner! [Get Back Up!]

When I cried out, You answered me, and made me bold with strength in my soul. (Psalm 138:3, NKJV)

Her eyes were like flames of fire that pierced my very soul. Out of all those people in that packed auditorium, how could she know those were the very words that I so desperately needed to hear?

As our eyes locked, she said, "Get back up ... Get back up!" but it was as if she sensed my resistance, so she hit me harder this time with the words, "You had better get back up!" and I broke.

I broke.

Tears welled up in my eyes, a big lump swelled up in my throat, and it felt as if I had been punched in the gut.

I broke.

And inside I acknowledged that I broke.

I was like a fighter down for the count. I was in the ring hearing the final count. With my last bit of strength, I felt like I was lifting my head, and from swollen eyes, I could see my trainer, my coach, screaming, "Get back up! Get back up! You had better get back up!" Suddenly, out of nowhere came this amazing strength to fight again!

I felt myself getting back up from the inside out. I could hear the roar of the crowd clapping and rejoicing as a new enthusiasm began to sweep through that vast auditorium. And, in my mind, I could envision neon signs flashing the words, "WINNER ... WINNER ... WINNER."

Has there ever been a time in your life when you felt defeated ... unsuccessful ... couldn't see the bright light at the end of the tunnel? Ever wondered when a change was going to come? You might even be asking yourself, "When are things going to turn around for me?"

Have you ever needed a coach to tell you to, "Get back up!"

Well, today, I'm your coach, and I am telling you to, "Get back up," and get back in the fight until YOU WIN!

You have the strength to WIN. You were trained to WIN. Now is your time; Go for the WIN!

Notes

Stay in the Hammock

You will guard him and keep him in perfect and constant peace whose mind is stayed on You, because he commits himself to You, leans on You, and hopes confidently in You. (Isaiah 26:3, AMPC)

As we meandered down the tourist packed streets of Nassau, an impression came so strong in my heart to take a quick spin through the brand new Pandora jewelry store.

Yes, shopping, and all the women said, "Amen."

Now, I've seen those shops all around the world on my travels but ehhh, I just have never been interested in the jewelry they sell. That was until this particular day. Isn't it funny how we can have no interest in something until the God part of us is alerted to it?

Some time back, I had been troubled by, let's say, "life." [I know I'm most likely speaking to the perfect peeps right now. You know, peeps who have had an easy life. But for the others ... who have been 'knocked-down' or maybe even 'knocked-out' by life ... I'm whispering to you ... as the perfect folk walk on by.]

In that moment, when I realized I was His child and that He cared for me and my life ... my 'hammock' experience began! TOTAL peace covered me as the cares of life fell gently to the ground because I was snuggled up in the 'hammock,' in His garden, with the One I love and the One who loves me. Ahhh ... such peace.

You, too, are His child, and He cares for you. Will you come to the garden, climb up into the 'hammock,' and be at rest where it's easy? There's plenty of room. He's waiting.

In the 'hammock' with the One I love (there's room for you).

(P.S.) In the Pandora jewelry store in Nassau - I got a charm with a 'hammock' between two palm trees ... He's good like that!

Notes

When Things Aren't Working [Just Breathe]

"I have come that they may have life, and that they may have it more abundantly."
(John 10:10, NKJV)

Ever had a time in your life when nothing seemed to be working [or at least working right]?

We've all been there at one time or another ... no shame in that.

It can be described like feeling as if you are a rat in a maze, a square peg trying to fit into a round hole, a hamster on a wheel ... just spinning and spinning with no end in sight lol!

But then, someone comes alongside you and breathes fresh life into you. Small words of encouragement ... a helping hand with a daily task ... an understanding smile ... an "I got you" ... simple yet life-giving to the receiver.

Encouragement from others instantly takes us from breathless to refreshed, clears our mind, and reenergizes us for the task ahead.

Will you walk beside someone today and be their fresh air?

Notes

Three Lessons I Learned from Five Little Boys

"Occupy till I come." (Luke 19:13)

When I saw those five little pups running, playing, and sleeping stacked like playing cards, I responded like any busy—I already got several pets person would—"No way!" To that little nudge deep in my gut, I said, "No way!"

"Who in the world has time for ANOTHER furry friend," I thought. I already have one inside the house and one in the backyard.

You probably guessed by now, right?

Something happened to make me change my mind. That something happened to be the yard boys revving up their mowers and lots of other scary, noisy, grass cutting equipment. Why that noise caused those little pups to run and howl with fear.

My heart just ... just ... melted ... like butter on a summer's day ... plum melted.

So, the rescue began.

The only problem was that I WASN'T acquainted with training, in my eyes, WILD, FREEBORN, MALE dogs!

For me, it has always been little, furry, eight-pound, girl dogs, that loved to wear pink bows in their hair, with an attitude of hurry up and give me a bubble bath, kinda dogs.

I was scared!

Scared of them. Scared of me. Just scared!

I worked up the courage and corralled them into the backyard. Because I knew I was in over my head, I prayed, "Now what Lord?" Obviously, I needed help with this situation, so I pondered what to do next.

Like a stroke of genius, I remembered one of my favorite TV shows. The one hosted by Cesar Millan. "That's what I will do," I thought, "I need to become a dog whisperer just like Cesar."

So, I ordered his DVD and trained to become The Leader of the Pack!

Like magic (not really), his methods and wisdom worked.

Soon I had five, little, freeborn boys thinking I was their mother and in total control. They didn't seem to sense how overwhelmed and sometimes fearful I truly felt. But with daily consistency and repetition, all the hard work paid off. Those little, almost full-blooded labs were brilliant!

That Cesar Millan, aka the dog whisperer, sure knows his stuff!

Over the years, I've had to say goodbye to all my loveable, brilliant boys aka friends. But from them or because of them, I have learned a few valuable lessons from God.

From the boys I learned:

1. Never disqualify yourself from a God-given assignment because He will equip you with whatever tools you need to be successful.
2. Your love boundaries can and will expand to include people/places/things that you never thought possible before.
3. When it comes time to let go, God is there to challenge you with an even bigger assignment.

Jesus shared a story in Luke 10 where a nobleman gave money to his hired workers.

He told each of them to take authority of what he had put in their hands and make it increase.

After a long journey, the nobleman returned, having acquired even more property.

He checked to see who had worked the assignment that he had assigned.

Much to his satisfaction, he found some who had increased that which had been given. But sadly, he uncovered one that was too fearful to work and increase that which had been entrusted to him.

The nobleman's solution?

Reassign the 'fearful' worker's assignment to the 'fearless' one that just went for it.

Question: What are you doing with what you have been assigned? Have you overcome fear to complete your assignment?

Notes

Convo' between Friends Is Sweet [Like Candy]

There is a friend who sticks closer than a brother. (Proverbs 18:24, NKJV)

Ever had someone in your life 'who gets you'? Someone who is 'just easy to be around' and them stopping by for a little chat can turn into hours of 'catching up'?

Everybody needs one or two of these people in life ... in fact, finding one in a lifetime is actually a rare achievement [one might say].

Sometimes ... no spoken words are needed. Why ... a glance ... a sigh ... a nod...or a wink...can convey a world of thoughts, feelings and secrets to this one...the one who 'gets you.'

And thinking about this 'one' sharing your innermost secrets is just missing from the colorful portrait that your friendship has painted.

This 'one' can make you smile with ease and dry your tears so that no stains remain.

Yep, conversation between friends is like candy. It satisfies, energizes, and gives you a boost [a second wind].

Today, will you be the 'one' for someone else? Maybe it's your turn to ...listen...to encourage...to understand...to just ...be there.

Notes

My Pleasure [She Said]

Pleasant words are like a honeycomb, sweetness to the soul. (Proverbs 16:24, NKJV)

What a journey! And all I remember one thousand-and-thirty-six miles later is ... she replied, "My pleasure."

I read recently that our IQ isn't really what makes us successful in the marketplace, keeps us out of jail, or even away from addictions. It's simply this ... the learned ability to "share, cooperate, and show kindness."

Earth-shattering simplicity, isn't it? Funny how everyday life can prove it.

While recently on a road trip, my growling stomach and I decided to lunch at one of my fav places. Smelling the breakfast as it sizzled in the skillet and listening to the clinking of dishes as they were moved, I followed the hostess to my seat. "Wow, what a packed house," I thought! To me, it seemed as if everybody and their brother was out for breakfast! And there in the back corner was my table just waiting to welcome me. "Ahhh, food time at last," I thought. But NO! The table next to me had a situation going on which resulted in an angry parent removing an unruly kid from the restaurant. Well, with the exit of the fight went my desire for food, any food, all food. So, I got up and left as well. Still hungry, and now with a little nervousness to boot, I walked towards the car with the feeling of ... uhhh!

While slowly walking and trying to shake off 'the situation,' I felt the Holy Spirit prompting me to remember the kind words that were spoken to me upon check-in at the hotel in response to my thank you for the room key. Simple words that felt like a healing ointment applied to a rough wound, a bear-hug from a friend, a touch from your mother as she pulls the hair from your eyes ... simple words, simply ... "My pleasure."

Those little velvet-lined words were healing for my soul. In an instant, the former situation was forgotten, and I was refreshed with a splash of happiness like cool water on a hot summer's day.

My thousand-mile, summertime journey has come to an end. Yet, I keep rehearsing those words that are tumbling in my head ... "My pleasure."

Have you ever heard someone respond to you with those words, "My pleasure"? Will you use those healing words today and be someone's gentle ointment?

Notes

Baptized in Love

He saw the heavens opened, and the Spirit like a dove descending upon him: And there came a voice from heaven, saying, Thou art my beloved Son, in whom I am well pleased. (Mark 1:10-11)

Words of affirmation. Words of approval. Words that confirm the love of the Father for His son.

Though these words were spoken thousands of years ago, they still vibrate with power and strength in the souls of man today.

As we read these powerful words, we can't help but be impacted with the intent in which they were released.

Ultimate approval. Indisputable love. Pleasure in the gift that had been given.

Because He came from a place of being loved, Jesus can love us, humanity, with an unending love.

Daily as we struggle with the need for forgiveness, healing, provision, and the desire to be loved, we find Jesus standing with His arms open wide waiting for us to receive Him, the answer to everything.

You and I are next in line to receive the same unconditional love that Jesus received from His Father. There is no more striving to be loved or approved of. We find that we are valued and loved by God just like we are.

Being baptized in the love of God is an awesome experience! Whatever love deficit you have will be filled until you overflow with joy. Your sorrow will turn to gladness, and your ashes will be exchanged for beauty.

My prayer for you today is that you, too, will know how much God is pleased with you and how He loves you with an unending love.

Notes

"Knock It Out of the Park!" [He Said]

Encourage and comfort one another and build up one another.
(I Thessalonians 5:11, AMP)

Didn't he know how tired I was? Was he aware that I had been burning the candle at both ends for weeks now? Did he know that I had a pain buried deep within my chest that throbbed like a toothache after eating ice cream?

Obviously not. But those were the words that spewed from his mouth as I pushed my tired body off my chair. I hoped that I could stand and give a somewhat coherent talk. A talk that would somehow encourage and motivate others to not give in, give up, or give out in this 'fight' called life.

Somewhere between his words and the push, everything changed.

I remember reading a story in "Our Daily Bread" that cited a recent study of 200k employees. According to "Our Daily Bread," these employees were interviewed and asked, "What is the missing ingredient that can make you more productive?" To my amazement, their answers were simplistic and directly to the point. These employees simply wanted to be appreciated and given affirmation from their superiors! This research concluded that receiving affirmation is a part of our basic human need.[1]

I acknowledge he is my superior ...

I acknowledge I was in need ...

And at the time, I didn't know what I needed but I knew I needed something!

And then those unplanned words rolled out of his mouth and off his lips. His words that stopped me in midair, like I was suspended, hanging between reality and unconsciousness.

"Knock it out of the park!" he said to me, "Knock it out of the park!"

For a split second, I turned and looked at him in utter amazement. Never had I ever heard those words of affirmation spoken by him to me.

I melted and became empowered all at the same time! And I LOVED it!

With one simple statement, and in a hair of a moment, I was energized, felt loved, and knew that I had the confidence of someone I hold so dearly.

Needless to say, it was a FANTASTIC night all around!

Instantly, because of his words, my tiredness was ... gone, just gone.

Gone ... was the wonder if I could do this.

Gone ... was the need to be affirmed by the one that I hold so dearly.

Gone ...

Like a volt of electricity, the audience became energized and encouraged, the host was thrilled with how the event turned out, and now I was recharged, revived, and renewed!

And it was all because of those simple words, "Knock it out of the park! Knock it out of the park!"

So, the research proved to be right.

As part of our basic human need, what will make us productive in any area of our lives is to feel appreciated and receive some kind of acknowledgement that we are capable and that someone noticed!

So, Dad, thank you for the words of encouragement that caused your girl to, "Knock it out of the park!" one more time. Your words give me life and makc mc want to do better, help others more, and enjoy every moment we have been given!

Notes

Believe - Dream - Love [This Could Lead to Dancing]

He that dwelleth in love dwelleth in God.
(I John 4:16)

Ever dance by yourself [and wonder if anyone is looking]?

Dancing is lively, rhythmical movement ... a two-step ... a waltz ... a break dance ... these all qualify as dancing, even tapping a foot can be viewed as moving to the music!

Then there's the heart of man.

Hcarts dancc ... bcat in rhythm ... experience joy, peace, and, best of all, L-O-V-E!

The heart that dwells or rests in L-O-V-E dwells in God [for He is L-O-V-E].

I become aware of when my heart is resting in His ... because

I begin to B-E-L-I-E-V-E that I can ...

I start to D-R-E-A-M even bigger than before ...

and I am dazed

by the expression of

manifested

L-O-V-E He has for me.

Which leads to dancing.

Because I'm aware that heaven has just shot me a download of fresh ... inspiration – hope – renewal!

LOL – a heart that is transformed by love can even cause you to dance through your kitchen and never worry if the neighbors will see you through the window ...

Heaven's remedy for the strain of life ... have a cup of tea and a cookie and just dance [and don't wonder if anyone is watching].

Notes

When Life Goes Gray [Splash Some Color on It!]

When the Lord brought back the captivity of Zion, we were like those who dream. (Psalm 126:1, NKJV)

You know the color that's not dark or light. It's just [blah] [bleh].

Ever felt the color? I have. Icky! It feels like the disappointment of a balloon that just won't hold air; the "I love you" that you long to hear but never gets spoken; better yet—the laugh-out-loud you do hear when you dare to break free and just 'go for it' ... (ha ha ... this is sooo Elaine from Seinfeld, but then you youngsters wouldn't know that old show, now would you?).

I can hear George and Elaine complaining now to Jerry at "The Diner" while eating the 'BIG Salad'....

Then Jer would remind the crew— "Hey! Life's not gray. It's COLORFUL. Just s-p-l-a-s-h it!"

"Just s-p-l-a-s-h it? Just like that Jer ... Just s-p-l-a-s-h some color on it?" — They would whine through their noses as they bashed their foreheads on the table.

Then it would sink in ... as Kramer dramatically glides into the seat next to them and drops some wisdom (from only the Lord knows where) — by saying —

"Yeah, just color it! Everybody's life goes gray! Everybody's! Like when the air is squeezed out of your dreams because 'stuff' doesn't happen quickly enough; and no, love doesn't always come easy; and yes, just believe and know you are going to make it through the situation!"

While adjusting his glasses, George would whine and ask, "But how Kramer, how?"

Elaine impatiently would step on George's words and pipe in, "Yeah, so Kramer, you make it sound just s-o-o-o easy."

Jerry, the leader that he is, would motion for them to just – calm – down and then he would lean forward and say—

"You could be like Winnie the Pooh or Piglet and have so many inflated red balloons that you float through the Hundred Acre Woods not knowing where you'll land ... but dream big anyway."

"You could be like the black cat who got the white stripe down her back and Pepe Le Pew thought she was the skunk for him ... muah, muah, muah ... but love passionately anyway."

"You could be like the little, yellow chick who thought he was a chicken hawk and was always trying to drag Foghorn Leghorn ("I say there, I say there, little fellow") home for dinner ... but just believe in yourself anyway."

Jerry's words surprised you, didn't they?

Moral of the story — when life goes gray and tries to bring you down, just s-p-l-a-s-h some color on it!

Dream BIGGER — Love MORE — Believe ALWAYS

Will you, like Pooh Bear, hold on to the balloons anyway? and Dream?

Will you, like Pepe, snuggle even though you are being pushed away? and Love?

Will you, like the Chicken Hawk, keep trying until you achieve what you want in life? and Believe?

... life will be more colorful if you do.

Notes

Your Uh-Mazing Life Now [It Just Keeps Getting More Sweeter]

Draw near to God, and He will draw near to you. (James 4:8, NKJV)

He demonstrated what LOVE looks like ... with that demonstration of LOVE came a shelter of protection and security that no one person or happening could ever penetrate.

No depression, abandonment, loneliness, or rejection can or ever will circumvent the LOVE the Father has for His sons and daughters ...

"His sons and daughters?" you may be asking. Yes—you and me.

This perfect LOVE of the Father towards us, his children, can't be bought or achieved.

It's FREE.

FREE because of one man named Jesus who paid it forward for us all.

When He, Jesus, paid it forward for you, He instilled inside of you intrinsically your worth and value as part of His family. Your true self and identity has its roots in your Father God.

So, your thoughts and input are valued in the conversation at the dinner table, decisions about tomorrow are shaped with you in mind, and there's always a place called home that is waiting to welcome you.

Because of Jesus, you are in the family ... protected ... loved ... welcomed ... valued.

As a new day approaches, know that Gods got this! He has an uh-mazing life prepared for you – with you in mind. He already knows everything about you, and He loves you just the way you are.

You are beautiful to the One who made you. Beautiful to the One who cherishes everything about you. Beautiful to the One who is always with you and will never leave you.

Just beautiful.

So, as you start to dream of all the new things you'll encounter in this coming season, remember ... all your days have already been sprinkled with amazement and wonder by the One who created the heavens and the earth ... simply uh-mazing ...

Notes

His Love Satisfies [More Please!]

"Before they call, I will answer; and while they are still speaking, I will hear."
(Isaiah 65:24, NKJV)

I had a friend who was in the middle of a pretty intense transaction. A transaction that would change her life for the better, and in reality, would profit me a little too. Her situation would change, and that would make her 'really happy,' and because I was there for her, I would benefit by 'being a trusted friend.'

I actually thought the entire set of circumstances were about her and what she was going through.

Little did I know how aware of the situation God truly was and how His thoughts about everything were so different from mine.

I say different because I found out He was watching how I behaved and the motive of my heart as I prayed for and encouraged my friend along life's journey.

He was listening. He was watching. Me.

Me. He was examining my heart as I helped a friend in need.

Upon waking one morning ... I heard so clearly ... God speaking to me ... about me ...

I thought God would be downloading me with the solution for my friend, right?

Nope. Instead, He whispered, "I didn't do what you expected but I sure am going to bless you!" And then He let me know when to expect the blessing.

With His whisper came unexplainable excitement and anticipation! Joy overwhelmed me as I began to weep.

Weeping because as I had laid down my life to pray and seek God for someone else, He saw and fulfilled my need before I even ever asked.

Now that's love.

Pooh Bear got it right when he told Piglet, "Love is not spelled, it's felt."

I felt God's love in a tangible way that day. Love that surrounded me like a warm blanket on a winter's day. Love like a mother's embrace that can make all the hurts of life go away. His love that would fulfill my need while I was seeking Him to help someone else. Now that's unconditional love.

Just like He promised to me on that day, He delivered! My blessing came and brought with it great delight because I knew that God really did care about me.

I want to encourage you, as you selflessly go the extra mile for others, put in extra time on the job, and stand with your family, know that God is watching and waiting for an opportunity to bless you beyond your wildest dreams. He is the God of more than enough, and He cares for you!

So, in this season of love's expression, stop and wait for His warm embrace.

He's your healer, your savior, your strength, and your provision. Trust that He is watching and listening and that He cares.

Notes

The Power of the Seed [The Life of Jesus]

For God loveth a cheerful giver. And God is able to make all grace abound toward you; that ye, always having all sufficiency in all things, may abound to every good work: (As it is written, He hath dispersed abroad; he hath given to the poor: his righteousness remaineth forever. Now he that ministereth seed to the sower both minister bread for your food, and multiply your seed sown, and increase the fruits of your righteousness;) Being enriched in every thing to all bountifulness, which causeth through us thanksgiving to God. (2 Corinthians 9:7-11)

I continue to be amazed by God and His magnificent ways! I see flowers blooming and feel the days getting warmer as I await Resurrection Day!

I want to share with you a practical application on the life of Jesus and the power of the seed from my book Waltz with Me. The following is what I taught my students on the power of one life; a seed:

As an elementary classroom teacher, the students and I always had great fun with our science lessons. We were especially excited about growing our own little garden. Our little garden simply amounted to paper cups filled with soil that were placed on the windowsill. But that was alright because from that little seed in a cup, a harvest was produced.

Now it didn't start out as a bumper crop. On the contrary, it started out as a bean in a bag! Teachers are very resourceful, and this science experiment was no exception.

The students and I pooled our resources and came up with the necessary tools to be a farmer for a day. We got our sandwich bags, a brown paper towel, some water, a shoebox, and found a dark spot to put all the "necessaries" in. Each student got a bean, placed it on a wet paper towel, and zipped it up in a plastic bag. Then we stacked all the bags in a shoebox and put it in a dark corner ... and waited ... with expectation.

It's amazing what happens when you leave the seed in the soil. Why in just a few short days, our bean began to "germinate." As it germinated, it sprouted a root. As soon as the root was showing, we transplanted it to a paper cup filled with potting soil. And there we left it on the windowsill. With the right amount of water and sunshine, the root began to grow down deep into the soil and a "seedling" began to burst out of the top of the soil as it reached for the sunshine.

Each seed has a designated number of days till germination. Every seedling has a designated number of days until it grows into a plant. And every plant has a designated number of days until it is developed enough to produce a crop or harvest.

When the fullness of the crop comes, it is then time to gather the abundance of the harvest.

The same is true with our faith. Our faith is alive. When we plant a seed of faith in quality soil, an expected harvest is sure to come. Why even a second grader can say, “Amen” to that.

Notes

The Art of Living Equals Loving

Being confident of this very thing, that he which hath begun a good work in you will perform it until the day of Jesus Christ.
(Philippians 1:6)

Faith, hope, charity, these three; but the greatest of these is charity.
(I Corinthians 13:13)

Though I speak with the tongues of men and of angels, but have not love, I have become sounding brass or a clanging cymbal. And though I have the gift of prophecy, and understand all mysteries and all knowledge, and though I have all faith, so that I could remove mountains, but have not love, I am nothing. And though I bestow all my goods to feed the poor, and though I give my body to be burned, but have not love, it profits me nothing. (I Corinthians 13:1-3, NKJV)

Strong words from I Corinthians 13, the so-called LOVE chapter of the Bible. I call it my goal chapter!

The 'Art of Living' implies that there is a flow to our life's path or journey.

Being Spirit-led is the passionate desire of the believer's heart.

Our heart wants to go 'home.' Back to the place of the warmth of the Father's embrace. Yet, He asks us to LOVE in this pilgrimage that we are on, until we see Him face-to-face once again.

The Father's expectation of our expression of life is that we illustrate the canvas of our life with the colors of love.

And what does that look like? It looks like faith that believes He is aware of every part of our lives, hope that He alone is the answer to all things, and to know that His love is all-consuming and limitless with possibilities.

So today, as we engage in life, let's put on love, like a coat, a garment that is worn. A coat that covers all our inability to love, to understand, to be patient and kind. A coat called Jesus who understands all the things we go through in life, and yet He lived His life with us in mind knowing that today we would rely on Him and His ability to overcome this world with all of its trials and difficulties.

So now you know, my goal in life is to LOVE more. Will you join me and make this your goal too? Will you flow with God as He orchestrates your life? It's the 'Art of Living' or should I say, 'Art of Loving'?

Notes

Forgiven [It Feels So Good]

For thou, Lord, art good, and ready to forgive; and plenteous in mercy unto all them that call upon thee. (Psalm 86:5)

Our paths hadn't crossed in many years. He said, she said, we said. Abrupt endings, lingering conversations, and unanswered questions all lay like china on a table set for a dinner party.

Endings.

An ending of our friendship shrouded in misunderstandings, loss, and hurt.

Would we ever recover? Would we share our life experiences again? Would we be happy for each other ever again?

Questions.

Questions that I never wanted to answer to be completely honest with you. And from the feel of things, I couldn't sense that anyone else was seeking the answers either.

Dormant years passed without expression. Suppressed emotions found themselves packed beneath layers of unforgiveness. Selected forgetfulness some may even say but unforgiveness nevertheless.

Until the day we met again.

By this time, many years had passed, and life had taken us both in different directions. But one thing remained ...

Our unspoken ending.

Who would be the first to bring "it" up? And by the way, what exactly was the "it"?

Tiptoeing lightly, we both genuinely enjoyed our lunch, the light conversation, and, yes, each other's presence until the years that had been walled off began to overflow their banks.

Like a gentle rain, unfinished conversations, unanswered questions, and perceived misunderstandings began to mist the air that we both were breathing.

I could hear the words that were being spoken to me but that wasn't the way I remembered our ending. I could hear the words that were being spoken to me but that wasn't the way I remembered the way I acted or responded oh so long ago.

Or was it?

To truly forgive ourselves, and someone else, one must look through someone else's eyes and see through the lens of their perspective. When we do, it's easy to realize that there are both real and imagined misconceptions and hurts. This day, I realized that misconceptions can cloud our vision and make it murky and hard to clearly discern and see the truth.

At first when we talked, I wanted to defend my point of view and how I perceived the death of our friendship. The death that had happened so very many years ago.

As I looked through the windows of my distant friend's soul, I saw what my friend was seeing. I heard the words my friend heard. I saw the actions my friend saw oh so long ago, and I wept.

Had I been so wrong? Had I acted so unkindly? Had I spoken those words so harshly?

From my trembling lips came the words, "I'm sorry. Will you forgive me?"

Gently, I felt warm hands on my face, and I heard these words, "It's all okay because I love you. Sister."

And I felt, oh so FREE! And she felt, oh so FREE! And we felt, oh so FREE!

Forgiveness is liberating and brings so much freedom with it that you want to jump for joy!

Question: Are there unspoken words between you and friends that are waiting to be said? Will you be the first to say them? Will you be the first to ask for forgiveness and give forgiveness?

I promise, JOY is waiting on you when you do.

Notes

Why Am I Here? [Destiny Whispers]

"I am the vine, ye are the branches: He that abideth in me, and I in him, the same bringeth forth much fruit: for without me ye can do nothing." (John 15:5)

It seems to reason, that humankind has one silk thread in common.

It's when we inhale one of those deep, cleansing breaths and ponder ...

What is this thing called "life" all about? Why in the world am I here? What's the purpose in all of this?

Those were my exact, meditating thoughts that tumbled over and over in my heart as I searched for a restful night's sleep. (Puzzling enough, those of us who are mindful of God and even those that are not so mindful, all ponder this age-old question.)

As my eyes began to fill with sleep, I drifted off and encountered an amazing night vision where my destiny began to whisper and be revealed to me.

As I share with you what I dreamed, be encouraged to not dismiss your dreams so quickly because

God could just be trying to reveal something to you that's amazing about your own life.

In my dream, I appeared in a vast auditorium, stage left. An associate I immediately recognized greeted me. He took me on a tour of a facility that, apparently, I was or about to be steward of. We made our way down some steps into an altar area and crossed over to the other side of the stage. There I could see a media command center where a team was working on editing video footage. The cool part was that everyone there knew me by name! Seeing all of this flushed me with excitement, and I felt like I was getting a glimpse of and even being propelled into my own future! I felt like DESTINY was letting me see what my future was to look like.

Then, instantly, I was alone.

I now found myself in the center of a stage at the bottom of steps looking up. In the center of this stage was a dazzling, bright light that shone on a violin. This was no ordinary instrument by any means. It was extravagant! Such craftsmanship. Its color was so vivid and rich looking. I quickly realized that this violin was suspended in midair! Nothing was holding it up. Not knowing what else to do, I reached out to take the violin in my hands while thinking, "Should I try to play the violin?" But before I could reach the violin, I heard a commanding voice say, "You are not the violin. You are but the microphone that magnifies the sound of the violin in the ears of the people, and you are to keep your instrument in working order."

I awoke with ease and an understanding, an impression, that DESTINY was whispering to me. Somehow this little glimpse had revealed to me what I was here for ... a worshipper that releases the loving heart of a heavenly Father to His people.

I pray, as you rest tonight, that you, too, will have an encounter with your destiny. That you will know why you are here. That you will know what your life's purpose is and how you will bring Him glory in the earth.

Notes

Little Prayer, Big Results

"That they all may be one; as thou Father, art in me, and I in thee." (John 17:21)

"Dear God,

Please help me to align with your perfect will so that I might walk out my assignment in the earth today.

In Jesus name, I pray, Amen."

That was my prayer as simple as it seems, yet, instantly, I felt a rush of strength and positivity like a jolt of morning java hitting my veins.

I'll admit that the reason for this prayer was because I was tired, a little frustrated, and, well, I just wanted to correct someone else's thinking to be honest.

Little did I know that God was working on me, not on the other person. See, it's not really about us fixing anyone else. Is it? It's really all about letting God align us, our mindset, with His perfect way of seeing our humanness, our humanity.

As our Abba (Daddy) God, He sees us as His children whom He loves with an unending, unstoppable

LOVE. A LOVE so deep that it cannot be exhausted or drained. His LOVE simply has no end and endures forever!

Well, on this particular day, I'll admit that I needed to line up my attitude with Daddy God's perfect way of seeing things!

So, I decided to ask for help as I said my wee little prayer.

As I asked for help with this day, immediately things became clearer to me as compassion welled up in my heart for the other person. I could instantly see their point of view and understand how hard they were trying to work through their own situations in life.

And then ... I started to let go ... let go ... from the inside out.

As I let go, I immediately noticed that I began to relax. All that irritation that I was just experiencing suddenly slipped from my emotions as my happiness and strength levels returned.

I was amazed; simple amazed. How could such a tiny, itsy-bitsy, wee little prayer have such dramatic results?

It was then that I realized that I had just had a life-altering, learning experience with Daddy God, who was now teaching me right in the situation I was in.

How cool is that? A simple, short, honest prayer

that yielded quick, tangible results and just for me.

What a teacher. What a teacher He is.

After this encounter, I felt like I could once again help my friend that was in need of a listening ear, a gentle heart, and genuine smile from me.

My entire demeanor changed as I once again began being there for a friend.

So let me ask you, the next time you run out of patience, or want to change someone else's way of seeing things, or simply run into a situation that is beyond your control as you are walking out life, will you consider using my little prayer that has such big results?

I give you permission today to use the tiny, wee little prayer that He gave to me.

Today as you pray, be amazed as peace, strength, and understanding instantly download into your inner most being, and you, too, once again are able to walk through the chaos of life with more compassion and patience than you ever have before.

It works. A little prayer with big results.

Notes

Make This Day, Month, Year—the Best Yet!

For I know the thoughts that I think toward you, saith the Lord, thoughts of peace, and not of evil, to give you an expected end. (Jeremiah 29:11)

"So shall thy barns be filled with plenty, and thy presses shall burst out with new wine" (Proverbs 3:10). That's the blessings that come when you honor the Lord with your "substance and the first fruits" of all your "increase" (Proverbs 3:9).

Proverbs, chapter 3, is filled with treasures of blessings when we put God first. So, as we expect a wonderful day, month, or year, we are assured that God has great plans for each of us.

God desires to direct our path this new season according to Proverbs 3:5-6. I read that we are to trust in the Lord with all our heart and lean not to our own understanding, and in all our ways acknowledge Him and he shall direct our paths.

That's a promise that He'll keep. When we trust and lean on God, He will direct us in life so that we make the best decisions and walk-through life humbly with our Father God in control.

Today is the perfect time to take a break from the usual pace of life and set our face toward God and ask for direction for our lives. Answers and direction flow in abundance when we rest in the arms of our good, good heavenly Father.

Lean into God, and He will direct you in all your ways.

Notes

A Small Little Gift Gave Big Love!

"God so loved the world, that He gave ..."
(John 3:16)

Round. Yellow. Smiling with sunglasses on. There it was just sitting there, smiling back at me.

I knew what was ahead of us. Hungry, hurting, and forgotten people. Yet, tonight seemed as if tomorrow would never come.

For snuggled up in the pillows on my bed was Smiley. That's the name I gave my gift. This cute, little, round stuffed smiling pillow would be called Smiley.

Smiley was a gift from my roommate who was sharing her room with me for the night. You see, tomorrow we were headed to the mission field to help those who couldn't help themselves. But for tonight, we were both grateful for a clean room, an inviting bed, and a warm meal.

As for Smiley, well, he was an expression of love. That's what I felt when I looked at him; just love.

I held Smiley in my hands, and as I brushed his

yellow fur back and forth, I thought, "Isn't it interesting how something so small, child-like, and unexpected could bring such a warm tangible feeling of love?" Then I realized the expression of love I felt was actually coming from the one who surprised me with the gift.

The one who was sharing her room with me. The one who was traveling to the mission field with me. The one who was investing her time, energy, and effort in helping me fulfill my assignment was actually the one who was the giver of love.

And then I thought of how our heavenly Father gifted His son, Jesus, to us that we might know He was thinking of us, that He was delighted to call us family, and that He joyfully awaits our return home. And then I felt really loved.

Sleep came so easy that night as I snuggled up in the deep covers and burrowed my head between the pillows. And just as my last prayer was said, I took one last peek to see if Smiley was still beside me smiling as he always does.

Notes

I Will Remain Faithful to My Faithful Friend

"Greater love has no one than this, than to lay down one's life for his friends ... I have called you friends." (John 15:13,15, NKJV)

Several years ago, Jesus asked me to lay down my life for Him. At the moment, I didn't really understand what that meant but my answer was yes. Now here we are together, years later, and my life can simply be summed up as a daily walk with Him.

While pondering this daily walk with Jesus, I came across this devotion by Oswald Chambers which describes this condition of life more eloquently than I ever could. Please be blessed as you read these words that were pinned so long ago as you, too, enjoy your daily walk with your King. – Paula

Wisdom From Oswald Chambers

"Jesus does not ask me to die for Him, but to lay down my life for Him. Peter said to the Lord, "I will lay down my life for Your sake," and he meant it (John 13:37). He had a magnificent sense of the heroic. For us to be incapable of making this same statement Peter made would be a bad thing— our sense of duty is only fully realized through our sense of heroism. Has the Lord ever asked you, "Will you lay down your life for My sake?" (John 13:38). It is much easier to die than to lay down your life day in and day out with the sense of the high calling of God. We are not made for the bright-shining moments of life, but we have to walk in the light of them in our everyday ways. There was only one bright-shining moment in the life of Jesus, and that was on the Mount of Transfiguration. It was there that He emptied Himself of His glory for the second time, and then came down into the demon-possessed valley (Mark 9:1-29). For thirty-three years Jesus laid down His life to do the will of His Father. "By this we know love, because He laid down His life for us. And we also ought to lay down our lives for the brethren" (1 John 3:16). Yet it is contrary to our human nature to do so.

"If I am a friend of Jesus, I must deliberately and carefully lay down my life for Him. It is a difficult thing to do, and thank God that it is. Salvation is easy for us, because it cost God so much. But the exhibiting of salvation in my life is difficult. God saves a person, fills him with the Holy Spirit, and then says, in effect, "Now you work it out in your life, and be faithful to Me, even though the nature of everything around you is to cause you to be unfaithful." And Jesus says to us, "...I have called you friends...." Remain faithful to your Friend, and remember that His honor is at stake in your bodily life."[2]

Notes

Leading with God, Awaken Your Giant Slayer

What time I am afraid, I will trust in thee. (Psalms 56:3)

In ministry, I have looked to God's word to direct and guide me in His ways of leadership. As I study, I have found that David truly was a "man after God's own heart." David was a son, a tender of the sheep, a warrior, a king, and a priest. All of these positions taught him how to lead with God, and when the situation called for a giant slayer, he was the man.

I read through David's life and found four key elements that I believe to be leadership characteristics that served him well. Please allow me to share them with you and may we all follow David's ways as he was after God's heart.

Here's what I found:

1. David practiced until he was self-confident and skilled. I Samuel 16:18 tells us he was a cunning player, valiant man, prudent in matters, a comely person, and the Lord was with him.

From this I take that I must practice my giftings and talents until God uses them for His glory.

2. David used self-talk to encourage himself. I Samuel 30:1-6 tells us that when he returned from war to Ziklag, everything was gone and burned. The people who served with him rose up to stone him. David encouraged himself in the Lord, and the answer came to him on what to do.

From this I take that I must say what God says about me and my situation, not what I think about it.

3. David stayed positive. I Samuel 18:8-9 tells us just the opposite of this. King Saul was a non-example of staying positive! We find the people rejoicing because David has killed ten thousand and Saul his thousand. This song displeased Saul, and from that moment, he "eyed" David and thought he was trying to take his kingdom from him.

From this I take that I must see accurately what God is doing in my life and go with His flow and remain positive.

4. David looked through his own eyes and believed that he was a conqueror and could do the job at hand. I Samuel 17:34-37 tells us the resume of David and how he killed the lion and the bear and how he believed he would take down the uncircumcised Philistine!

From this I take that I must see my own success as God sees it and know that through Him, I am able to get the job done.

Four giant-slaying leadership keys learned from the life of David. I pray you find them as helpful as I did.

Notes

Revelation – Visitation – Habitation

Show me thy ways, O Lord,
teach me thy paths. (Psalm 25:4)

As I recall the life of Esther, I become aware as she engages in relationship, that should we follow her path, we, too, can end up with the heart of our King.

Young Hadassah, Esther, once found herself isolated, abandoned, and overlooked. But all that quickly changed for her when she determined herself to flow with the destiny that was now calling to her. This destiny, her destiny, had the capacity to seek her out and draw her into a life with the King who would prove to be a powerful protector, provider, and nourisher.

Her path, our path, to the King begins with revelation.

Revelation is revealed knowledge, understanding, and wisdom.

Esther understands what the King desires when she puts her trust in the eunuch who knows the King better than anyone else. Like Esther, you and I trust the Holy Spirit to lead and guide us into all truth so that we understand how to yield our will to the perfect will and desires of our Father God.

Secondly, Esther's path to the King's heart led her into an encounter or visitation.

Visitation is an encounter that has a beginning and an end.

After soaking and preparation for nine months, Esther was summonsed to one night with the King; a divine encounter. You and I, too, prepare ourselves for time with the King when we soak in worship and give Him unabandoned adoration.

Lastly, Esther finds herself chosen to be Queen and companion to the King.

Habitation is when relationship is bound in commitment to each other.

Esther found herself with the heart of the King when all her desire was focused intimately on him. He was now the object of her affection, and she was now his. His to love, protect, and provide for. When we focus our attention intimately on Christ, our King, our heart fills up to capacity and overflows with Him and Him only. The issues of life fade, distractions fall away, as the audience of One permeates every inch of our heart-soul-and-mind.

Esther and her life reveal to us it really is possible to find yourself ignored by the world and yet, at the next moment, able to capture the heart of the most powerful ruler in the nation. Her life's story reveals the path to the King's heart through wisdom (revelation) and an encounter (visitation) which produces a dwelling place (habitation).

Esther, a life lived that shows us how understanding leads to one night that equals a lifetime.

Notes

The Note

Eye hath not seen, nor ear heard, neither have entered into the heart of man, the things which God hath prepared for them that love him. (1 Corinthians 2:9)

I recently received an email from a heartbroken friend asking for prayer.

Heartbroken because she had poured herself into others and had received what she felt like was little in return.

Her note to me read something like this: I am evicting a family today. It has been heart wrenching for me. I helped this family for the last two years, loaning money, buying gifts for the kids, and taking them to church, and the list goes on and on. They stole my heart as I thought I could help but I found that last month's rent was used to buy drugs. The eviction is today, and as I drove by last night, I could see the two-year-old child standing looking out the window as the dad was putting a mattress in the back of a van, and I just sobbed! I have prayed so hard and feel that I have worked so hard to help these young people have a better life. Today I feel like a bit of a failure and sadden by the fact that I poured so much into their life. Please pray that this family will be taken care of and remember me as well.

My eyes watered when I read her words.

I wondered what would happen to this family. I questioned if they realized all the help and concern they had received from this dear friend? My mind raced through several scenarios where I myself had helped many in so many different ways, and I pondered the end result of each attempt that I made to make life better for each one.

I realized the outcome for each may be different, but the underlying principle is the same.

It boils down to freewill which is a voluntary action to choose.

I applied my friend's email to how our heavenly Father must feel when we use our freewill to choose a life that is not surrendered to His son, Jesus. Our Father, through Jesus, has given us the path of life. A life that is filled with joy and peace, provision, and protection. And yet, some choose to not follow this path of life and meet with self-inflicted pain and sorrow.

I prayed for my friend today. I prayed for this struggling family today. And I want to pray for you today. May you come to know the loving arms of protection and provision as our heavenly Father reaches out to you today. He's there! Will you receive all the love that He has for you?

Notes

Your Seed Can Produce an Unusual Harvest

And other fell on good ground and did yield fruit that sprang up and increased.
(Mark 4:8)

Who would have believed that this simple, southern girl from 'nowheresville' would one day be sitting on a sofa in the home of one of God's greatest "Generals of the Faith," Dr. Oral Roberts!

My, I was a crybaby! I couldn't help it. As soon as I drove up on the property and started heading for the door, the tears began to flow. I was moved deep in my spirit because of the magnitude of the moment. "God's General of Faith!" I thought only people like Benny Hinn, Rod Parsley, or Bill Johnson would be allowed to sit at Dr. Roberts' feet and receive a blessing of impartation. But not me! Well, yes, me! When you have been asked to "waltz" with the Master (the Bridegroom, Jesus), you never know where it is that He is going to lead. There I was, a handmaiden, dancing with an awesome God who led me to one of His most influential representatives. And it can happen for you too!

You see, it was because of Dr. Roberts that my family knew about "seed-faith." My Granny always watched his programs, read his books, and supported his ministry. For many, many years, she sent a "widow's portion" to help hold his hands up. I can still hear him say, "God is your source, so give, and expect a miracle."

How true that is!

Just like any science classroom experiment with a germinating seed, there is an expected outcome of a harvest. A harvest is that which the seed produces when the time is right.

Apostle Paul was such a great teacher. In 2 Corinthians 9:6-11, we find him teaching on the seed and its production. He says, "But this I say, He which soweth sparingly shall reap also sparingly; and he which soweth bountifully shall reap also bountifully. Every man according as he purposeth in his heart, so let him give; not grudgingly, or of necessity: for God loveth a cheerful giver. And God is able to make all grace abound toward you; that ye, always having all sufficiency in all things, may abound to every good work: (As it is written, He hath dispersed abroad; he hath given to the poor: his righteousness remaineth for ever. Now he that ministereth seed to the sower both minister bread for your food, and multiply your seed sown, and increase the fruits of your righteousness;) Being enriched in every thing to all bountifulness, which causeth through us thanksgiving to God."

I believe you and I, with our lives, are the bountiful sowers Apostle Paul was referring to and a mind-blowing harvest of realized dreams is just about ripe for the gathering! Amen.

P.S. (Dear Granny, all these years later, your seed-sown made room for me – thank you.)

Notes

Endnotes

1. www.odb.org/US/2013/09/10/the-power-of-affirmation, accessed 6/17/2022

2 www.utmost.org/will-you-lay-down-your-life/, accessed 6/17/2022.

Prayer

Father God,

Thank You for showing up in our everyday lives. Help us to trust You as You use the small ordinary things to teach us such valuable lessons. As we walk through life, we ask You to be our guide both day and night. Our eyes are upon You and our hearts trust in You. Show us our purpose as You help us to fulfill our destiny. Let our hands be Your hands in the earth and our feet always on Your path of righteousness.

In Jesus' name –Amen.

About Paula

Paula has always loved being a teacher and inspiring others.

At a very young age, she had an awareness that God was real and that He wanted a relationship with her as her loving heavenly Father.

As Paula grew in relationship with God, she discovered in His Word spiritual truths that have impacted and dramatically changed her life in many ways.

Because of her passionate life with Christ, Paula has gone from shy to courageous, timid to confident, fearful to fearless, and she wants you to know, "So Can You!"

Today Paula is an inspiring, passionate, prophetic leader who pastors, travels, and teaches, both nationally and internationally.

She has authored the book, *Waltz with Me*, and her first children's book *Itzy and Bitzy Learn to Share*.

Paula is an anointed woman of God who has a passion to release the presence and glory of God in the earth as she ministers prophetically in word, song, and the "gifts of the Spirit."

Paula's Spirit-led ministry uniquely communicates God's powerful prophetic message that crosses culture, gender, and the nations. She enjoys calling the coastal "Low Country" of South Carolina home.

Books by Paula Douglas

Waltz with Me

Learning to Draw Closer to the King

Have you ever desired a closer, intimate relationship with God? Are you trying but question yourself and ask if He really knows I'm here?

In Waltz with Me you will learn practical steps to implement that will bring you into an intimate relationship with God that you have never known before.

Itzy and Bitzy Learn to Share

Twin Shih Tzus Learn a Valuable Lesson

If you desire to teach your children how to share using God's word, then this book is for you.

Follow along as Paula's adorable pups and their yellow dinosaur teach this valuable lesson.

www.ingramcontent.com/pod-product-compliance
Lightning Source LLC
LaVergne TN
LVHW010105110826
845155LV00028B/495

* 9 7 8 1 9 4 9 2 9 7 7 6 8 *